Caming My Life

Caming is the metal banding that joins panels of glass into a unique design.

When I first heard this word I loved the image of broken or cut pieces of glass being brought together with metal to create a stained glass window. My experiences, my connections, my inner thoughts are how I got here now. These are the camings connecting all of the beautiful and not so beautiful aspects of the stained glass that is me. This is the "pane scape" of me, a never finished life! A reflection of color, light and various elements. It is a work in progress and continues to call out to light so it can reflect its creator.

Being confronted with non-existence, allowed me to fully live. Thoughts of death? They let light in. When light hits glass, beauty reflects outward.

This is simply a collection of moments from my life. These are the pieces of glass that are me. (The beautiful, the mundane and down right primal.) Bringing them together to honor and on some level acknowledge my life. Caming it, if you will. My family members and friends may not know my inner life. I hope to reveal its light and its darker corners and perhaps, affirm for me (and the reader) the blessings and the beauty of what is here right now for all of us.

Frank Asher

YOU BE YOU!!
I'll BE ME!!
YOU DO YOU!!
I'LL DO ME!!
FREE TO BE YOU!!
FREE TO BE ME!!

Written by Frank Asher

Artwork for cover and installation for publishing by Dorian Charis.

Editing assistance

David K Stewert...And several other friends.

Along with special mention to Editor, Walter G. Meyer

Thank you all, for helping me finish this particular art project of
 my "reveal" of sorts.

Connections

A real life story..(Thank you Cassie)

She asked if that was my pumpkin down the street lying next to the curb.

She had seen it on the vine the day before. We went out to look.

It was "my" pumpkin.....A tire had smashed a piece of it.

I had noticed it missing the evening before.

It was growing on the street side of my fence.

It was a glorious heirloom pumpkin suspended in the air while leaning into the chain links.

She slowly picked it up and carried it with such gentleness and respect.

There was honor in her action.

She carried it back to my garden from whence it came. Now it was on my side of the fence. She walked over towards the mother plant and asked where she could put it. I suggested she lay it right on the ground below where it once hung.

And there it sits....Seeds exposed. Very much like the mother did last fall.

This one is early to pose for regeneration. But who knows what nature has in store.

It's funny! I had stories that came up for the missing pumpkin.

Having lived in the city for so long, I assumed it was stolen.

My friend suggested that someone's fairy godmother came into my garden to whisk it off

to be used as a carriage. I liked that. I'd be honored if a fairy god-mother was roaming in my garden.

However, the way it was settled in the gutter, it looked as if the stem snapped, the pumpkin fell to the ground and rolled across the street settling near a car tire. It certainly was getting big, it would have the power to roll.

Gardens have always taught me about birth, life, death, renewal...Ever since I was 4 or 5, I learned about seeds. I saw how some plants survive, thrive, and some not, while they're growing in the same garden location. I saw how some plants bear lots of produce and others only one or two...Nature's fate...

Nature is a miraculous thing. When I watch it and listen to it, I am the wilderness.

My War Lord

There she was!

She spoke with a baritone voice while flipping her lavender and purple hair away from her frail shoulders...She cackled at her bubbling brew of words..

When she spoke of the winking demon, her perfect pearly whites were on display.

"I am just putting this in the mix", she said. She said that a lot.

I wondered how many words have been boiling in that ever changing cauldron?

How long has she been spewing provocative sayings and potions out to those who were not afraid to converse with her? Cause when people spoke back, she could pluck their words right out of the air and dress them with a spell and mix them in her pot. Giving them a whole new meaning and context.

She'd take a moment to see if you noticed her magic act.

"There is no such thing as being vulnerable to love. The word vulnerable is about war.

If you are vulnerable to love, you are possessed...Did she just wink?

I swear, whenever I heard her speak, I'd thought I was hearing a man. Yet, I'd turn around and see her impish face and silver/lavender curls and her purple lipstick.

She was all female...Meaning, she knew her masculine self as well.

She had tongue twisters to proclaim. She was a wordsmith for sure.

Her sister/friend talked about hope in the dark night of death.

She only chuckled and said: Let me see what comes from this...

The dark knight? No? She paused...Hope is the dark night. To find hope in that night, one can bring a new day...

"Be available to the mystery," she proclaimed with authority.

Hmmm...She was feeling tired. I bet she had thousands of incantations to share.

But for some reason her cauldron was cooling...

What's in that pot anyway? Would she mentor others in creation?

Deep down, I felt the world needed this sultry voice to spin phrases, sentences and universes into our spinning non static reality.

New dimensions, new realities, new realizations, all needed.

She knew her gift and her place. Time to stir the pot, she thought. So quietly, she tended to her brew...She will speak soon...When the words fail others, she will grab them and turn them inside out.

...Keeping us all moving and turning toward the mystery.

Ode to Mary Oliver

Oh Mary,

Your words hold me. They have buoyed me.

I also know of the quiet hunter you refer to.

You challenged us. Your words continue to challenge me!

Oh Mary,

I now know I am both bride and groom to this life.

I married JOY and GRATITUDE recently.

I wore a 12-foot-tall wedding dress while surrounded by millions of tulips in Amsterdam.

Oh Mary, Thank you for reminding me of the geese.

I live in a deeper place when I hear them.

Oh Mary,

I do hope to meet you on the other side or at that threshold to what's after this.

Bev. 03/22/2019

Today I breathe.

You...no longer.

Your compassion and love is missed.

Today, I remember our love. I know you do, too.

Today, at this moment, I am not sad.

I am so grateful, friend, for what you are to me.

What you will always be to me.

As long as I breathe, I carry our friendship.

When the moment comes for me to breathe no longer,

I hope we meet up.

Today, I breathe.

Today, I move, dance on the earth.

Today, I laugh.

Today is what I have and you don't.

I know you want me to enjoy it. Our talks were REAL.

Our conversations, deep and true.

We were complete.

Thank you for being my friend.

My Dream Man

I saw him talking...He proclaimed with a smile: "I don't want adjectives with my coffee!"

He slowly walked by, stopped and turned to read a paper on the counter...

Maybe for two "minutes of forever."

During that time, I saw exquisite maleness. Body strong. Arms, thighs, and glutes of testosterone.

Black wavy hair and a trimmed black beard.

My thoughts: Wow, simply divine masculinity.

He must have known I was eying him because he was on show...I was enamored.

This wasn't lust. This was an appreciation of beauty, strength, and appeal. Okay, it was lust.

He turned around to head towards the front of the cafe and slowly turned his head to me and said HELLO!

I said hello back and immediately felt he must have heard all the longing in my soul.

My chest had a burst of life.

I periodically looked at him, watching him read his phone at his table.

As I got up to put on my jacket to leave, he looked at me and suddenly looked away.

Was he just scoping me out? Was he being shy?

I walked past him towards the front door to leave.

He looked up and said, "Have a good one." At least that's how I remember it.

I put my hand up like the white man saying "how." And said some gibberish.

Oh, I hope to see this man again.

For Ron!

September 1954 - February 2009

I will take my last breath in due time. Until that expiration, I MUST remember LOVE!

If tonight were my last, know that I am grateful for our short time shared.

To alter my grief?

I would place a flower on a rock, a feather on a piece of bark and my hand on my heart.

I would smile in my breath having known you.

Sometimes, sadness can teach us to dance with joy, gratitude and abundance.

Your eyes ~the mystery~ the finite, that is illusion...

I see you and know all is right.

Sleep today. Rest and lay down your worries.

Dream of no more pain; where spirit moves in plain sight and LOVE rules.

You have shown me strength in the singing heart!!

Can I sing you a song?

Who are you?

I've been put in the most difficult position.

Forgiveness!!

To be truthful, can I forgive? Can I offer *MERCY??*

You have shamed me with your lies.

No strings attached.

Until you webbed a prison of deceit.

"I do not want to risk losing your friendship."

Were those words deceitful, too?

You have put me in the most uncomfortable position.

I hate you for that.

You don't care for me.

Moving from the center, I have seen many things.

Your lies, my frailties, my truth.

I am alone with my truth.

How do I use my anger?

I need to move outward with it.

You are lucky.

I could kill your smile. The longer you wait...

The less chance there is for anything.

(To this day, I do not remember who this is written to)

Magical Boy

Just a day ago, I rode the ferry on rainbow waves.

My destination? Almost forgotten.

My intention; to reintroduce my 55-year-old self to my younger self.

This boy flew above physical abuse, sexual molestation and body shame.

He knew NO MATTER WHAT that his magical heart would prevail.

This older rendition of me needs to get reacquainted with the power of play and magic.

A big thank you to the younger one!

Two of Us

Hope and Missy...Watercress and Bittersweet

They have received radiated light to save them.

They both got a lot of stuff.

Mobiles of rock and wood.

Pots, plants and inspiration

Simple little hoarded things from years gone by.

Tiny trinkets of memories all around

Things for projects of creation waiting in the wings.

One is in a relationship.

The other is in one with himself.

Hope and Missy...Watercress and Bittersweet

They have received radiated light to save them.

His Hope passed one day and he was set adrift.

His Missy expired days later leaving her master in moments of lost
hope.

Both creatures were euthanized.

Both humans were/are floating like mobiles in the wind.

They both rise to not euthanizing their feelings,

But to give meaning to them.

Time is measured for both.

One might hold more fear than the other.

One might be the other's friend.

In that case, both are friends in one way or another.

Hope and Missy...Watercress and Bittersweet

They have received radiated light to save them.

One has been deprived of hormones

The other is on small doses of LSD and Psilocybin. Both are using

cannabis.

A glass of red wine and or a gin martini is always a good thing.

Both swimming through air while taking walks in the cold woods.

One has numbers of years in his head. Actually, they both do.

But one would rather feel the moment and let the numbers be out

there in the breeze somewhere.

Which one goes first? No need to ponder that.

Both will continue to move on and up.

Hope and Missy…Watercress and Bittersweet

They have received radiated light to save them.

One mostly gives and the other practices receiving

And at times parodies the other.

Their energy is in full view.

Both see connections and the lack

Each feels the other's movement.

One walks a lot and other one does breath work and yoga

One eats lots of pasta, the other one practices fasting~then eats

pasta.

Neither one wants to lose dignity.

Hope and Missy…Watercress and Bittersweet

They have received radiated light to save them.

A letter to Cancer

To Cancer:

At first I thought I'd start this letter, "Dear Cancer".

But, I have mixed feelings about thinking of you as dear to me.

On the one hand, I have received an overflowing amount of gifts that my mind could never have imagined. That hand has been doing its best to hold those gifts close to my heart.

On the other hand, well, let's say that hand is ready to slap that first hand silly.

Because with these gifts comes fear. With these gifts, comes anger. With these gifts comes apathy.

Not sure if fear, anger and apathy were already inside me, or if all of that was triggered by robotic surgery to remove my prostate, or 44 radiation sessions to my prostate bed or the removal of 48 lymph nodes or the 2 weeks of bicalutamide, or the 2 months of abiraterone and prednisone or the 6 months of Eligard.

Or maybe it was the simple phone call I got from my Urologist in 2017?- "The bad news is, "You have cancer".

The reality is that my brain, my testicles and my adrenal glands have all been shut off from producing testosterone. Imagine this; the testosterone in this cisgender body, which makes me male (not what makes me a man) has been depleted to a negative three so that you can starve to death. Because if you do not die, word has it you could take my life.

The rest of my body has been impacted by the removal of my prostate. The rest of my body has acted out because of these chemical/pharmaceutical invasions. The rest of my body has been grieving a loss. A loss of what I do not know how to bring words to.

Hot flashes, cold flashes, muscle spasms, bone ache, brain fog, depression and fatigue have swirled all about me. It is as if my body has separated from all that I know to be.

Sitting here right now, I ponder...Perhaps I need to be acutely aware of that?

What am I without my body?

Well, I have discovered a will greater than I thought. I have a will to keep moving along the journey to health. A will to let go of fear, anger and apathy in a nanosecond so I can come back to the present in gratitude and joy. A will to move past the people I have disappointed or have disappointed me and simply LOVE them. I now see a deeper connection to how I can become a different person, a better human. And trust, that is a daily job because my apathy is very stubborn. Sometimes, I'd rather say, "Fuck it" than allow myself to be human.

Dear Cancer,

Are you like the friend that quickly comes into a person's life, and then leaves having changed them? I have changed. That is undeniable.

Hey Cancer...I am now engaging with my body, mind and soul to rid you ...

Shrink, die, go, get out. GET OUT!!

Though you may be a part of this body, your cells are flailing.

I see your worth and I know what it has cost me.

Thank you for visiting.

My whole body, mind and soul say with the sound of 1000s of megahertz,

WE RELEASE YOU! YOU WILL GO NOW! BE GONE!!

A love letter to a sunflower

My love.

Though I claim you as mine, you are not.

You are your own...I simply planted a seed, watered it and watched you grow.

You got off to a slow start and then mid-June, you started to grow.

By July you were over 10' tall with a glorious sun full of promise and adoration.

I could tell you worshiped the sun and the moon...It's only natural.

Now, I see a heaviness approaching. Your flower is hanging low, and it leans forward towards the morning light.

Your movement is not as fluid as it once seemed.

You do not travel east to south to west and back again like you once did with your daily, wild, abandoned dancing.

Your flower, which was once my shower head to wash away fears, is now heavier.

You carry a heaviness for the future.

I must learn from you, my love.

I want to live as if I can be wild and dance forever because I want to.

But that is not the truth of how life happens.

I do want to lower my head gracefully to the morning sun.

To LOVE and trust that my life will have moments left behind like your seeds.

Thank you, dear sunflower. I Hope to see parts of you next summer...

I hope for the future.

Meanwhile, I will dance as lovingly as I can...I am sure I will step on some toes.

Like we all have for eons...

First Day of Summer Solstice 6/21/2020

I love to harvest faith in my garden of hope.

I revel when I am barefoot and can feel forgiveness on the balls of my feet and in between my toes.
I breathe! I inhale JOY into my expanding lungs, I hold it, then release it and I carry it down to earth with gratitude.

My heart dances when rain comes along. I am my skin, and my skin is right next to it all.

Time becomes eternal. The present moment is full.

My psyche blooms toward the sky with wonderment.

My blood flows in sync with the chirping birds, the lightning bugs and the buzzing bees, the night crawling worms, the budding seedlings and the fast climbing vines.

My fingers and thumbs can receive all earth's gifts leaving me all muddy and tranced out.

I love! I live. I forgive. I am reborn. All of me is seasonal and perennial.

Right here. Right now. This breath.

This view; while pulling weeds out, and letting go of thoughtless thoughts, under the tall flowering stalks, presents me with such abundance

I love my garden of HOPE. So much to glean.

It is still LOVE

My body knows of the love that dare not speak its name.

My body knows of the many that have even become nameless in the four decades of exploring that love.

But now! Now, with you, a love that has not found its name is flowing through my body.

My heart, my mind revel in this delightful joy you bring into the room.

My nose, my eyes, my ears tell me you are love.

You are near me, yet so distant.

I dare not speak this love aloud for I fear you will run.

So, I let my nameless love, my unspeakable inspiration run through me.

I say I love you inside my heart. Yet, those words are not the love I want to share.

I love the idea of running my hands across your tattooed abdomen.

I love the idea of bringing my nose up to your pits, your neck, the crown of your full head of hair.

I love the idea of a kiss to see if your lips would swell with joy.

I love the idea of a nipple nibble to see if ecstasy would move through you.

I love the idea of you running to me and releasing all of your fears, pains and worries onto my body.

I would stand strong on this earth, in this love, and hold you.

This love is all that and more. But I dare not speak it, name it. Or call it out to you.

All I can do is show you in silence.

You may either feel it, speak to it, or if I am fortunate, you will honor it. Even if it's from a distance.

It is a love that you dare not recognize. It is still LOVE. My love.

Morning love.

I love when I wake up before the alarm.

I love how a cold water rinse wakes up my whole body after a hot shower.

I really love a cold shower!

I love the sound of the coffee maker dripping.

I love the silence that surrounds my house in the early morning.

I love this day.

I love being alive in this body right now.

This love will continue long after this body stops breathing.

I love the cancer that decided to present itself in my body.

I love the radiation that is ridding my body of this cancer.

I love my breath. I love my friends. I love those who have rejected me.

I love those I perceive as enemies.

Now family, that's a harder pill of love to swallow.

I am learning to take that medicine.

Questions

Would it be out of line to proclaim that we all want

to be loved or to love? (DEPENDS ON WHO YOU ASK.)

Am I out of line when I believe I am walking the line?

There is always someone out there ready to change me,

Ready to control my direction, or even make me edit my words.

Or is that all me?

So hey words, help me.

Let my words be an instrument of peace, like Saint Francis recites.

Words, let me not be afraid of the mess, the betrayals, the attacks, and projections that can appear after my truth is spoken and before peace arrives.
Mind, let peace reside before I speak.

Heart, let my feelings dwell in love.

Soul, let my spirit see beyond the words.

Even when I hear the profane, let me be in place for healing,

redemption, forgiveness, and LOVE!

To be

I am not Shakespeare.

But I know of that place between "To be and Not to be."

Sometimes, it is vast, dark, and filled with terror.

Sometimes, light and love emerge and I am ready to receive the

moment.

I have no partner, no children and my family is distant
geographically and on occasion, far away~spiritually and emotionally.
I have friends and loved ones around the world and I eat too many

meals alone.

I have been told I am stubborn, yet many times I feel weary, wimpy

and confused by compromising.

My life could be a Telenovela. A soap opera with flair! There's been

love, loss, pain, suicide, murder, molestation and abuse. Yes,

extreme drama! Oh, and honest in your face surreal humor...And lots

of SEX!! (I really miss sex.)

XXX

Getting Physical.....WARNING...(THIS IS SEXUAL in NATURE)

I want to have SEX.

I want to forget and remember.

I want to caress, kiss, suck and fuck so I can feel my body.

Fuck me so I can lose my worries.

Massage me so I can get inside my body and out of my head.

Let me fuck you so I can gain some control. I want to dominate my fears.

Let me dominate you. I want to smell your ass.

I want you to lick my ass so I can moan with pleasure

Instead of spinning and sighing with anxiety.

Make an agreement of unspoken words to fill the void that all
my demons create.

Put your cock in my mouth and let my tongue swirl around with
delicious thoughts instead of my paralyzing thoughts.

Pinch and suck my sensitive nipples. Create for me pain and pleasure.
Replace the pain of worthlessness.

I want to breathe deeply and exhale all of the toxic patterns inside of
me.

If your touch is good enough, I will want you to do it again and again
until we both collapse in ecstasy.

Then, I can remember my body can heal.

Fuck me...Yea, that's it...Oh yea, that feels good.

I WANT TO FEEL GOOD.

Yea, that's good...Not anxious or depressed.

Yea! Yes, lick my balls and finger my ass...Get it wet.. Yes. Now I am
ready!

No Boundaries

I have given myself away not recognizing where I begin or where I end.

I am not sure how I even got to give cause I really didn't get that I had value.

Then, my value wanted to trade, barter and exchange and so the giving became an unconscious business.

Now, I have to give it all away.

I have nothing that I can see.

I ask: How can I serve?

I ask the ether, "How can I offer, what can I offer?"

The MOTHER...Yes, the capital M MOTHER says "Go with the flow."

The beloved is sometimes awake, BUT

I, we, you, me, are floating through this universe and we bump, we scream, I lose sight like the beloved.

Not realizing my giving - not realizing my gift is just in being.

Revelation

This morning I accidentally splattered hot grease on my belly.

"Shit!" I said out loud, It hurt!

I was flash-frying shishito peppers for breakfast.

I then ate one and got back into turning the peppers.

I then remembered something from the past, from the late 1970s.

I had been ironing a shirt for work and I was fantasizing about a gorgeous man.

He was always kind to me when he visited my work. I so wanted to date him.

While in my daydream, I suddenly rubbed my belly with the very hot iron. Shit, I said.

It scarred my belly in the same place where I now have grease burns.

Right when that iron hit me in 1979, I punished myself for the sexual thoughts I had for this handsome, kind man. I thought, "Oh fuck, god is burning me to deter my hellish desires."

How long has my psyche carried that?! Imagine that?!

Now, 40 years later, I say "shit," and get back to my peppers.

I have no more time for self-flagellation. No more time to torture my gay soul.

Now, this grease burn has a relation to liberation of the decades of mental bondage.

Delicious shishito peppers by the way.

On the Road

My life could be simple, meandering thoughts of a man almost ready
to go.
These thoughts lead me to another...And another. And another.
Will you come and be with me?
Let's go for a walk.

It is something else

I do my best to revel in the moment of now.
Listening deeply to this body.
So much so that I once missed my death bed.
Many times, the now has included a hot flash followed by a chill in
the bone.
A deep breath touches the conscious and I move into the future.
Total grace. Every day a grace makes itself known.
 Reclamation, redemption. Karma~Dharma

Family

Sibling Love

I cringe when you tell me you will love me no matter what.

Why? Cause I know you see me as a heathen. As a sinner damned to hell.

Nope! No thank you. Keep your love to save your own soul.

My soul is fine.

Thank you very much.

Thinking of you

Now, it is my turn to hold space and love for another.

Months, they say. Months until that final expiration.

Time will bring us gifts.

My mind will trust. Perhaps this most recent solitude was to prepare me for her.

LOVE brings HOPE and Faith to this time that is here right now.

Fragments of Family

I could tell you stories of murder, suicide, sexual abuse, physical abuse, and deadly car accidents because my family has had it all. A few fragments. My paternal grandfather, Revis, killed a man in the mid-1930s. His uncle, who was the sheriff, let him out of jail because a posse was coming for him. He fled Arkansas, leaving his family behind. Two years later, my grandmother packed up their four kids and met up with him in California. Grandpa became a violent alcoholic, and the family suffered from it until his last breath. My grandmother almost left him in the late '50s when he threatened to kill her with a gun. He was in pain because his daughter, my Aunt Betty, put a rifle to her head in 1958. My eight-year-old cousin, Judy, found her mother. When Grandpa got cancer in 1959, my grandmother went back and took care of him until he died in early 1960. I was 4 and I remember him. In 1962 my maternal grandmother was murdered by a man she had picked up at the restaurant where she was a waitress. The resulting shame and rage simmered within my family for a decade or more. My mother had a hard time with the fact that the killer got off just because my grandmother was a lonely, single woman picking up a stranger. The message was that she deserved it. Throughout the '60s my father had a drinking problem. So did his two brothers. Looking back now as a sixty-five-year-old man, I see the patterns. I have been near that edge, if not over it. There but for the grace of God…In 1979 my nineteen-year-old sister, Lisa, was killed in a car accident—only two weeks after my father found his mother dead in her shower. My parents were distraught, my father particularly beaten down. But somehow that tragedy created room for them both to experience their remaining three children with a deeper love. I felt the change, but it was a long time coming. Because of my sexuality, my father would beat the shit out of me when I was young. Once I passed out. Once I had to go to the hospital. Several times I went dead on the inside. Shame can do that. There were plenty of welts from a belt or wounds from a fist or psychological bruises from the words. Once he was so angry with me for playing house with the girl next door that he made me wear a dress and lipstick and walk around the room. He said that if I was going to play with girls, maybe I should be one. When I was twenty-five, I asked him why he had done that. He didn't remember the event. Today, I can only imagine the shame that ran through his veins. Family shame. It's in my blood, too—the "sins of the father" kind of shame. What does a son do with that? Shortly after my confrontation with my father, he gave me a blessing. At the time, I was exploring my sexuality, and I confessed to him that I didn't know if I wanted a boyfriend or a girlfriend. At first, he said he didn't like hearing that. But six months later, one evening after dinner, he put his hands on my shoulders and said, "Son, whatever makes you happy is what counts. Live the life you want to live." I am eternally grateful for that blessing. Shortly after, my father died of a heart attack at the age of forty-nine. I wonder if he said anything like that to my younger brother, Steven. Two years younger than I, Steven was a drug addict and alcoholic, like our uncles. Maybe if my father had blessed his other son, as he did me, the rifle would not have been put to his mouth.

Steven (as I predicted) committed suicide just before Thanksgiving 2014 at the age of fifty-six. His nineteen-year-old daughter found him. Generations of trauma repeat themselves. My mother and remaining sister became a whole other collection of shards and fragments—some filled with resentment, some filled with love's light. Love is complicated. Family is complicated. Especially when trauma and tragedy play their hands so sharply.

To this day, I carry my maternal grandmother, Marie, with me. She held space for the emerging gay teenager. She loved me, and I knew her love was genuine. That short time in my grandmother's kitchen in my early teens served as an anchor. I'm not sure how, but it carried me through the beatings, the losses, the dysfunction.

Family is love. Family is heartache. Family is rage. We carry so much in our blood and bones. And our ancestors see how we carry it.

Pieces of Me..

(Have you written your Obituary yet?..So many memories..)

Frank Larue Asher Jr...Frank Asher...Frankie

Born in Salinas, CA on Aug. 30, 1956, at approximately 7 pm PST

Final breath:__________

It's been a WONDERFUL LIFE! It's been fucked up also. The lineage is full of addictions.

The trauma and violence was/is rampant. At many moments, it flourished causing heart poisoning and mind fucking actions along with degrading and humiliating verbiage.

This, I internalized at some point...It is most likely in my DNA...I have worked at integrating and healing all that. I have had the luxury of time.

There have been several suicides in my life.

<u>One understandable:</u>

My cousin "Hottie" was given a colonoscopy and then a colectomy in the early 70's.

He just wasn't up to wearing a bag for life. So, he did himself in.

<u>One Unknown, but with lots of stories: My Aunt Betty.</u>

My dad's sister put a rifle in her mouth. Aunt Betty was a beautiful woman. Rumors of an affair. Talk of murder...Who knows...All of that is in the ether.

Everybody in my family came over to our house one day. It was either after the funeral day or the day everyone found out. I was about two years old.

I was outside in the sandbox/dirt plot all day by myself. I played with the grass seeds on the slide. I made mud balls. I made bricks of grass and mud...I sang songs...

Adults came out periodically to check in. Even a neighbor peeped over to make sure I was good...My mom brought me in that night and gave me a bath. It was the dirtiest I had ever been.

<u>One suicide predicted...My brother.</u>

I saw suicide in his head while he was driving me to the airport.

I knew that I could no longer speak to the truth with him. Two months before he suicided, I told my sister to get ready cause he had gathered all of his guns and disappeared for a few days.

His life was falling apart. Yet, all he could say was, "I'm good." I still don't understand why anyone would want to keep that gun...

My uncle gave it to him. I wonder if it was the same gun my Aunt used? My niece now has it. My brother's grandchildren do not know he suicided, but one of them will get that gun someday....It was something that Steven said about his drinking and drugging that shut me out completely.

I knew he was on the track to suicide. I did all I could...Especially when I was doing absolutely nothing. At that moment, I knew there was nothing I could do.

That's when the lineage of trauma kicked in. It was right in my face.I felt it under my skin and in my bones.

I am still here to write about it, so that I don't have to think about it...

Memory Field…Remembering my brother, Steven.

October 22, 2015

Cigarette smoke, a deep cough, a hack at least.

Fishing tackle, bait and the cold outdoors

Waiting, waiting for a bite.

Fish, the smell of trout coming out of the cold-ass lake in the early morning wind…

Damn, my fish is bigger. Not yours this time.

We get home to clean fish. The slimy scales, the blood and guts. The smell of earth.

And you say it to me LOUD, with your deep smoky voice:

"We are making memories, bro!"

There is an even louder silence within me.

My inner voice responds:

"Remember this one memory, because that is all he's got left."

That was a good day…My last full day with him. From 4:30 am till dinner.

That was a good day, my last full day with him…

Now, his ashes are in the lake.

Early Winter 2014

What I accept about all of this is that I have my life. I have my breath,
I can live for love, joy, and gratitude.

What I cannot change is that my brother, Steven, put a gun to his
face and pulled the trigger.

He just couldn't think of anything else to do. He was done with his
pain.

For Asher

(My great-nephew, born during Covid)
Always know this.
You are loved.
Many are around to help you discover who you are.
I will be there from afar.
I am 63. Who knows if I get to see you in person.
Know this. I have learned to love me. Despite what the world says.
If I were to die today, and come back in your body, I'd take these
lessons.

Life & Death

Who is this?

How did I get here?

I am astounded!

Sure, not perfect. But beyond anything I ever could have imagined.

Then sometimes, my reptilian brain kicks in and runs the show until I come back.

Where is it that I go?

Fear of death. Fear of not having enough. Fear of not being seen or loved.

I look for warm hearts and kind souls with light in their eyes to hold a place for me.

Then when I arrive, I know the reptilian narrative is false.

I treasure warm hearts and kind souls that have congruence in words and action.

These folks are my mirrors.

I can see myself and simply say I am amazed and in love with life.

I do appreciate it all.

To know sweetness, one has to know bitterness.

To know light, one has to have been in the dark.

To carry joy, one has to be intimate with sorrow.

To be fully alive, one has to engage with death. (Samo Samo)

DEATH

...Are you close? I feel you coming.

I will be seen as dead.

What can I do until then?

What can I take and play with while I am here?

What can I offer up?

What can I be?

Dying death!

My fear of death has to die.
I know it is eager to. Images of falling off balconies, or running off the
road or simply eating too much until I can't breathe, I know it wants
to leap, it wants to crash and burn.
It's desire is to expire.
Fear, do not fret. I will kill you. A sword, clean and swift, perhaps?
I will lay you to rest.
A ritual to release fear like ashes over the ocean's waves.
Or like the breeze carrying the finch in flight, time to exhale.
I say goodbye. I say farewell. I say thank you for making yourself
known.
In meeting you, I've come to know you closely and like many friends
that have betrayed me in the past decades, that I have said, "I am
done, or I am dead to you."
I now address you! Hear my heart.
This time, I say: "You are done!" You have done your job and now
you can die.
Now, going forward, Fear of Death shall only be a faded memory.
Now, I live life...Ashay

My Angel

I have to imagine that the angel of death is QUITE handsome.
He has to be carrying such beauty in order to snap me out of this
breath.
With eyes so lucent, to guide me out of this sight.
Hands so compassionate, that his touch would make me melt into
the ether.
With a voice so mellow and reassuring to ease all my fear of another
journey.
Yes, I know I imagine much. I am still here, still living here, before his
arrival.

More Angels

I made a bargain with five or six angels. I reneged on all of them, too.

Integrity is a miss. I wonder if they still follow me around?

I have witnessed my mother take her last breath. I assisted my friend
Paul in his final moments of living in his body. I then got to see a
baby girl slide out of my friend's vagina...It was as spiritually
invigorating as the deaths...Yes, watch a human die. Sure, grief is
present. But something bigger begins to reveal itself. At least it did
for me.

Yet, now...With my years showing up as finite, for some reason,
through all that and much more, I find joy and abundance all around
me. Sometimes right in front of my face. Even inside my
heart...Along with gratitude, connection, and Love.

Random

Having no thought to what time it is.

Though, I have asked myself the question, I ponder, reminisce, reflect, and remember what's been given to me.

Some of it, I've had no say in the matter.

Parts have a grand identity attached.

Identities can be fun, played with, and played-up even.

Identities can also be burdensome, heavy, and downright depressing.

Identities can be internalized, promoted, and stealth in nature.

Identities can give pause.

Identities can be of an organic nature: I do, therefore I am.

Identities can be worn like a winter coat or a summer V-neck.

Identities can be inked in for prosperity and eternity.

Identities can shape shift; floating in like an ancestor hovering over our shoulder.

Identities can be determined by the season in a person's life or manifested in order to survive a catastrophe.

Whatever identity presents itself, whatever large, floating bubble appears, know which identities you can use for service or to use for lessons.

Which part of you will embrace the next incarnation?

Disease. Cancer Survivor.

Suicide Survivor. Sexual Abuse Survivor.

Sissy Boy. Boy. Wimp. Man.

Son. Brother.

Fuck Buddy. Boyfriend.

Faggot. Gay. Drag Gender Fucker. QUEER.

Writer. Actor. Performer. Storyteller.

Alcohol Lover. Alcohol Abuser.

Depressed. Angry. Playful Fairy.

Gardener. ARTIST. Writer.

Cosmic Adventurer.

Lover.

Friend! (I love that one!)

Oops, I said it.

I said it out loud.

I spoke of a thought.

"I am afraid this cancer will take me out."

I said it. Oh god, I said it...I have thoughts of this possibility.

But then immediately, I rewire my brain and connect it to my heart.

Finger SNAP. All of my cells are in alignment to heal, to flush out disease, quantum metabolic change is activated.
I get back to what's at hand.

My breathing, my love, my gardening, my imagination and perhaps,

some magical thinking.

Saying it...Wow...I didn't say something that goes with that fearful

thought though.

I will say it here:

I wish you were here next to me in that quiet place, holding my hand

now and then.

Movement

When nothing wants to get done and when nothing seems to be the
place where I go,
I wonder what my body is telling me?
Sensations and movement get my attention.
Life is moving inside at a previously unknown awareness.
Fear and gratitude...Stillness/nothing/ALIVE!!

Homage to William S. Burroughs

I know what I want.

Chill to the bone.

Feel it right now in every atom.

Where does a person stand when the unraveling is happening to them?

I wish you were here next to me in that quiet place, holding my hand now and then.

How long has my psyche carried that?

You have (had) cancer.

Gardens have always taught me about birth, life, death, and renewal.

I love to harvest faith in my garden of hope.

We are not ALONE!

I move throughout the house while listening to the theme song of the movie, "Beauty."

Snow has fluttered in...ICY... Slippery.

The dog is napping after our walk.

Have you ever said to yourself,

"This is more than beauty?"

Have you ever said things to yourself that you reneged on?

So many synapses have wired and rewired themselves for over half a century!

Surviving

What brought me here? Have you ever asked yourself that question?

How in the hell did I make it to ______ ? (fill in the blank!)

For me, it's, How in the hell did I make it to my mid-60s in relatively one piece?

I mean, there are so many pieces really. Some pieces shattered. A few pieces were lost and never found. Some pieces recovered from a lost mental abyss. (All of those pieces are fodder for more fecund stories.)

Missed the Vietnam draft. AIDS missed me. Drunk driving never killed me. Got attacked and beat up once, it could have been worse. Got attacked another time, could have been way worse.

Like a butterfly, I have been contracting my body and moving through space with a wild, and glorious sensory system.

And yes, I made it here because of some serendipitous encounters, some serious falls and more falls.

I made it here due to the friends and despite other "friends."

You know what I mean?

Many moments during my waking hours, I can sometimes curse

I have learned a conscious intention to more often bless my journey.

This journey to myself has never been dull.

Mundane maybe, at times, uneventful, but never dull. Others may see me as dull. But my life has not been dull.

My self: "All that is ME," self

Fabulous.

Even, after I stop breathing, like millions before me stopped their breathing, like all of you that will eventually stop your breathing,

What is left behind when the final exhale extends itself never to return?

What essence will I offer and then selfishly take back and expire into the ether?

Just before my body expires permanently, what is left for the world? For this planet? For all who have been touched by me and my strange, over the top ways? Intended or accidental encounters, we have all been touched.

First, I leave behind my shame and guilt! I have wrestled and danced with these accomplices and many times have transformed them into self-love and care.

Or, have I just simply released them. Like dropping a pencil on a carpet.

I see glimpses of compassion for life's cuts in the belly, for the blows given upside my head. I am astonished at the full-hearted presence I call in when I engage with cancer. I can be munificent or obsolete depending on my mindfulness.

Procrastination

I H A V E SOOOOO M A N Y T H I N G S

I DON'T KNOW WHERE ANYTHING IS!

SO MANY THINGS!

SOOOOOOO MANY...SOOOOOOO??

Chill to the bone..

Have you ever gotten that chill in your bones?

Blood curdling chill?

That slight tightness in the chest. Slightness of breath.

Mild mental disappearance of the mind's moment?

Do you remember a thought in that moment of the chill?

I had one today...Bone chilling!!

The thought was just how fucking lucky I am to feel that chill right now.

When I consider how abusive I have been to my body over the last 40 odd years.

It is a wonder that some organ hasn't failed me already. (It may be about to.)

I would be afraid to look inside my body. Especially after 44 sessions of radiation.

Remember those pictures of lungs from smokers and non-smokers?

I get a chill thinking about my lungs, kidneys and liver, heart, and prostate bed...It is BONE CHILLING.

Hey body, I feel the chill! I am with you...

Unraveling

Feeling, Sensing, Witnessing the unraveling.

Speaking out loud to it.

I proclaim to the universe: "Things are unraveling!"

It's hard for me to stand still.

Where does a person stand when the unraveling is happening to them?

I'd suggest right in the middle of it.

Be in the eye of the storm…I will do my best to hold compassion for myself there.

Cause I can be the first one to beat myself up for not controlling something when I really don't have control. (Some things you simply cannot control.)

Once the mind settles, once my mind is in my breath, I get catapulted into the eye of whatever storm my fears have created…
If you looked at my living room, you'd notice that there have been storms. There have been high tides and winds. There has been a level of restructuring from the floods.

New rivers and streams. New patterns on the earth. New gardens.

Breath helps me a whole hell of a lot! The eyes of my storms are on higher ground and are partially protected when I breathe deeply and settle into the expiration. I hold on with the ideas of new blood cells traveling all through my body. I love mainlining oxygen.

Moving out broken useless thoughts along with the CO_2 and the fear of death.

I still have to wear protection, but I am still here now! Storm or no storm.

Destruction, reconstruction. Debris moves so slow sometimes.

Practicing gratitude for surviving storms instead of being pissed because the storms have messed up my house.

Phrases float through my thoughts...Verbiage swirls.

I have a reminder on my phone to sit and write those words down. Many times I simply snooze the button every nine minutes. No writing.

You'd think I'd feel better when I complete something once the alarm goes. Even if it's less than 10 words.

Perhaps as a test to my growth, I will write down 11 words when the alarm sounds.

I will give a place, mood and a few words so you can enter my mind.

No promises of perfection and beauty. Just an entry.

I think the most important thing is for me to enter that place.

I see the seasons pass. The minutes, seconds disappear.

When I notice my breathing, I get the finiteness. I so get it.

I will make that promise...11 words at my 11th hour -

HOPE, Spontaneous healing...Nature is calling...Holding expiration and gaining inspiration.

Balancing Act

Life happens. A love comes into our lives, and we make room.

A traumatic accident occurs and there is suddenly an empty space.

Words we carry in our heads keep us going...moving...floating through time.

Thoughts create an inner narrative, and we go with them. We think we are the creators.

Suddenly, we realize we carry other people's thoughts about us.

Life happens, there are regular random occurrences and reoccurrences. People come and go, jobs change, new pathways reveal themselves.

Serendipity appears and we ride with it.

It is all in the elements. We are living in them... Right here, right now.

Bliss

I have been able to carve out a living with my hands, my heart, and with dirt.

With Mother Earth herself...Working with the fairies to clean and plant life in tree boxes in a rich city that didn't see them. Guerrilla gardening is pure delight. Then a green space in Old City. Living and dancing with a GREEN BEATING HEART.

I have witnessed men transform right in front of me. Brain synapses firing new information of self-love and deep healing breaths. I carry that with me wherever I go.

The buoy in the midst. It has a bell to remind me of LOVE.

Whether someone reads these words out loud, or if someone reads these words on the printed page, ponder this.

We were here. We will always be here.

All of the millions of people, all of the animals, insects and creatures deep in the ocean or underground near the roots of plants-rhizomes and seeds even up into the air above where the buds bloom for new seeds.

All of us are here.

I have moved on...I am living the "happily ever after" life.

I have discovered gifts. I am still claiming new gifts.

I have run outdoors under a dark sky with a zillion stars shining on my sovereign.

Speaking to my deepest senses.

With fireflies dancing around me in my sarong, beauty has touched me.

This fairy has transformed and continues to do so.

Though my body lies cold and is without breath, this body has taken me on a journey in the here and now.

And for that alone, I am happy and grateful. Eternally grateful.

May you know the resilience of peace and the strength of hope.

May you find opportunities to release trauma and shame.

May love pound in your heart until your last breath.

Just a thought

Thinking about dying while having my coffee.

Yes, I know it will happen...and I know it will happen to ALL of us.

Then again, the thoughts.

How much time do I plan?

Who do I ask for help if it is slow and gradual?

Shit! This could be happening right now.

Cancer is silent and somewhat hidden.

Yet, it's giving out a signal of distress. I think!

I can feel something...Is it my body healing?

Is it my immune system attacking the cancer cells?

I want to find it. Heal it. LOVE it!

Then I want to toss it out of my body.

Cancer, I release you. I thank you and I will remember your lessons.

Is there anything else you want to tell me before you go?

I will do my best to listen and respond accordingly.

I will pull no punches with you. Your end is at hand.

I will outlive you!!

Hope

When a simple touch occurs when passing a cup of coffee and I feel a strong tenderness of energy, a mild vibration of HOPE...I feel good about starting the day and even better about sipping my coffee.

Cancer

"You have cancer."

My urologist told me over the phone the day before Thanksgiving.

I catapulted into a minefield of bombs, grenades, booby traps, barbed wire fences.

Mind explosions! Heart implosions!

My mind was in a war zone. So was the rest of my body.

I began to feel my body - **TERROR**.

I gathered myself up and stated out loud,

"I will navigate myself with as much grace, and mindfulness as possible."

"I will be my own medic on the front line."

I stumbled and fell rather quickly. I've stepped on some booby traps,

I have moments of selfish denial. I've bargained...I've shut down.

I have unconsciously tossed out truth grenades.

Bloody skeletons swinging behind the window shutters...Yep, those grenades.

Stained curtains. Too many rubber bullets, too.

I have also cornered myself in front of the mirror. And in front of others.

Truly though, I have additionally found a clearer grace, an expanded serenity, and a deeper self-acceptance.

Acceptance in so many new and everlasting parts of me.

Joy, Gratitude, and Beauty have made the bigger explosions. A BIG GIFT.

When you said, "I will support you in your battle with cancer,"

I stopped in my tracks and jumped behind the trees...

My breathing increased...Breathe in to the count of 4, Hold 7, Exhale 8

I then stepped out from the brush.

Is it really a battle now?

My relationship to cancer is different from a battle.

I liken it to a call and response.

Cancer calls out, I respond. Sometimes I will NOT hear of it.

I call out, and sometimes, cancer responds.

Cancer and I, me, and Cancer...It's a voice dialogue.

Living cancer can leave me if it already hasn't.

I know many who have lived with HIV and AIDS for decades.

I can follow them. I remember. I will carry my lessons forward.

I am in service as if I am a member of the Peace Corps.

I have my tools to regenerate as well as obliterate...So thank you, friend, for your support!

A far reach?

Today I sent the email.

To officially request to be a part of the NIH Study for Immunotherapy.

It is a fowl vaccine plus a chemical fusion to alert the immune system of cancer.

I just ponder!

How can the immune system miss this now?

In my mind I know where the cancer has been thought to be.

Surgery, radiation, biopsy, CAT Scans, Pet scans, MRI's.

Yet, the immune system seems slow on the uptake.

Cancer cells need regulation. They are cut out, sprayed/washer over with chemicals that are injected into the bloodstream.

Flesh is melted and bones are saturated by radiation light that is pinpointed by a computer. Such accuracy goes to a precise spot in the body. Up to 45 times in 60 days.

Yet, the immune system is blind and tone deaf to the invader.

Or is it? The immune system is perhaps hiding and waiting to pounce when the cancer shows weakness from physical activity and food alternatives, from sunlight and fresh air due to vigorous breathing.

My body is working at claiming itself.

Cancer was present before it was discovered. It had a chance to grow undetected.

Now, the body/mind intelligence is doing what it was meant to do.

I wonder if fear is a part of the immune system?

Does one part of the body have access to healing other parts of the body?

I can tell you this: Emotions can run the body.

I release my fear of not being able to control this journey and I will trust what's presented to me and I will be patient.

Patience. Patience Patience.

Random Thoughts

Crystalline prisms

They are mine!

My chimes! Oh, my chimes.
They have bothered many folk.
The sound that rings out in a deep tone of benevolence reverberates
to my bones.
I am calm...I am here and I hear.

WORDS (1)

That is what my to do list says: "WORDS"

Words...Words...WORD!

I have gone back on my word with the angels. I have told myself so
many things, so many times, so many words, so many empty words
that they fall lifeless to my aging feet. Those words have cut me and
hurt others. So many words

To have a word with you? To have a word with the one above the
angels, to ask for compassion.

To ask for clemency.

I can run around like the Tasmanian devil picking up all the littered
words.

I try to bury them. Hoping new meaning will sprout.

Hoping salvation will pop up and offer a smile.

WORDS (2)

I cast a spell so that every word that passes will be of love and affirmation.

The broken words are dead. It is winter. I will wait with hope.

Hope! That word is new life for me.

Hope, love, compassion, forgiveness, faith, patience, kindness.

There! Done!

 Words! Intention accomplished! More words to come! Be gentle to self.

House guests

Dear toxic sadness, disappointment, grief, anger, and discouragement,

I know you all. You've stopped in to visit from time to time.

I have greeted you; I have entertained you. I have sat and wallowed with you.

And then, you've gone your own way. Leaving me a bit weary...depleted...

But for all of you to step into my home together?

For all of you to bring sleeping cots, tons of baggage and groceries as if you are planning for the apocalypse? To bring uninvited, unwanted guests of disease and mortality with you?

Really?

Just know, though I hate to clean and organize, though I procrastinate in doing my work, your time has run out.

Expect eviction...

Expect a change in me.

My patience with you is thin.

My patience for creativity, joy, connection, meaning, and love has outlasted you.

I am making room...I will start at the threshold and go to the deepest darkest corners for light to do its magical duty.

Blessings! Good riddance.

And if the door hits you on the way out? Oops...

WORDS (3)

Words can create

Some defame, some annihilate.

Words attract so they say.

Which leads my mind to what I want to bring my way.

First, can we all agree on anything? Yes.

We all poop, pee, eat, and sleep? Not necessarily. Some humans breathe due to machines, or have catheters and bags to take care of things.

We all want something. (Usually.)

Naturally

Alone~Aloneness~Lonely

Alone time~Lone Wolf.

You've got to do this alone. You'll never walk alone.

Grief can be lonely~alone with grief.

The lonely hearts club. The Lone Ranger.

Alone again, naturally.

When we engage do we acknowledge each other in order to balance the lone scale?

We are born alone. (Sort of.)

We die alone. (Sometimes.) But then again, we are with the universe.

So, we are not alone after all.

Yet, it's a journey one can only take alone.

We are hardwired for social engagement!

That's what helps us survive~sometimes it helps us live longer lives.

"Wherever you go, I will follow you."

It's lonely at the top. It's just as lonely in the gutter.

We are not ALONE. Well, where are you? Will I be going this alone?

My journey had to be taken alone.

And yet, so many held space and heart for me.

This alone thing can SUCK...Mostly because it is a figment of my own making.

Making it alone doesn't really make it better~simpler maybe~but not better!

Being with myself doesn't have to be alone by myself.

BY MY SELF! I stand with my SELF!

That's a full, lovely and loving place to start

If I were God

If I were God, I'd change some things in the Bible.

Remember the verse, thou shall not make graven images of the Lord

our God"?

If I were God, I wouldn't give a shit if they made graven images of

me.

What would I care about?

I am GOD, you can't hurt me by your graveness.

 But I would put in its place, in big letters:

THOU SHALL NOT MAKE GRAVEN IMAGES OF YOUR FELLOW

HUMANS!

And all other LIVING THINGS.

Shame and Guilt

I See You. It is time for easy going love

Gratitude and whimsical joy, I hear you when my bones vibrate from

my humming.

We: Gratitude, whimsical joy, me and my bones,

We all rush and flow through this moving galaxy.

January One, Twenty-twenty-one

I am so grateful for my situations.

The man said appreciation has more energy than gratitude.

I appreciate my standing. Oh yes, I wish I had more.

Not necessarily more money, prestige or influence.

Though my socialization has trained me to go for more of all that.

More appreciation is what I want. Cause appreciation brings me right into the center of NOW.

Going forward in 2021. I want more of the now.

More NOW!

Not more right this instant. More in this instant.

I've practiced releasing thoughts, urges, impulses, limiting beliefs.

Releasing let downs, releasing missed connections, missed dreams.

Releasing brings me into the now.

Where breathing with my whole body brings my whole existence into the now.

Going forward, I want to carry all that I am and can be.

Exfoliating resentment, shedding self-loathing.

Exhaling lost love and pulling in new oxygen for self-love.

How about you?

Will and Surrender

Will,

I have done my best to deny you.

For I have only seen you as broken and lacking.

Once I embraced you, once I acknowledged you with my love,

You gave me strength and resilience.

Surrender,

I hated you. Many times, I am the last to hear you…the last to say

yes to you.

I have equated you with powerlessness; with my hands up in the air

and saying,

"Not you again!"

But something changed the last time you came for a visit.

For my will was on track and whole, so I could call out to you with my

loving heart.

Surrender, you have carried me all this time while I was broken and

deep in my darkness.

You were holding Will next to my heart.

Pardon me if I purge

...I know what I want to do...
I want to play in my garden WHENEVER it suits me.
I want to connect with friends by phone, Zoom or Facetime whenever we can.
I want to invite folks into my green space...Always have!!
I want to eat good homegrown produce and healthy organic farm meats and vegetables.
I want to live a healthy, joyful, loving life until I am at least 80...90 would be way cool.
 ...I know what I do not want...
I do NOT want to read and respond to that many emails anymore.
I do NOT want to have to hear your justifications for #45.
I do NOT want to hear "all lives matter" or "blue lives matter" or "we want a straight pride parade."
I do NOT want to see another rich man get richer and richer off the rest of us.
I do not want to see another Confederate flag. Period!!
I do not want to explain myself anymore.
The *"Want-do and don't-want dance."*
I DO want financial security...I want to share it...I want to see others have a shot at it.
I do NOT want to hear you talk about your religion...It's yours...If I want to know, I will ask.
I DO want to know how you connect to our earth.
I do NOT want to hear about life after death.
I DO want to know how you see your life before it ends.
I DO want your happiness to light up the mornings.
I do NOT want you to continue pissing all over other people's happiness.
 All of this may change later today or in 5 minutes.
But for now, I know what I want...And I know what I do NOT want.
It's my body.

My body has physical feelings.
Which ones are healing? Which ones are old pains?
Which ones are just an old body?

Which ones are harbingers of what is to come?
I shall breathe. I shall sigh. I connect to you and listen as closely as
possible.
I shall also be grateful for how my body is feeling.
I sit, I breathe...My tummy rumbles. I lay my hands to touch my belly,
my heart, and the channels in between my legs and torso.
I feel the currents of life at my core, flowing around my groin and
down my legs.
Exiting out of my toes.
My hands are my father's hands.
My feet are my mother's feet.
Except mine have been earthing all spring and summer.
Dry skin...brown soles...sensitive toes with old man nails.
They have sensed earth's energy, earth's love, earth's release,
earth's gifts, I imagine.
This body awareness is new, exciting!
Sometimes fearful.
I am feeling my whole body. I LOVE it!
My head gets in the way...A thought of expiring pops up to the
surface.
I breathe in to remind myself of the gift of life right now. And all is
well.
All will be well. All's well that ends well.

Nothing

Nothing. Nothing more within me.

Nothing between the blood cells, the neurons, the bones and ligaments.

Nothing between the molecules, the atoms.

ABSOLUTELY NOTHING.

But, POTENTIAL!

Even the "what-ifs" must reside somewhere near nothing.

This moment, I embrace nothing.

I breathe, I hear, I smell, I see, I feel. Oh, what is that?

It is more than nothing, or nothing more.

1995

Feelings of...
I once felt younger.
I am not young anymore.
I feel rage and jealousy.
But I am kind and giving.
I wanted to be the first, I don't think that I was.
Fantasies that I have spoken about. Perhaps you wanted to fulfill them but couldn't.
Doors began to open but you closed your eyes.
Polarities and extremes.

1996

Heart flowing, beating. Breath breathing. Years of experiences.
Many more to come. Pen in hand.
Eyes, ears ready...Ready to let go.
I am god-spirit.
Paper moving...Molecules swirling beauty.
Life. I am. Yes...I thank you.

Early morning magic (wink wink)

And, just like that, out of nowhere, all of a sudden, without notice, and for no apparent reason, the coffee pot stopped. It's broken, finished, kaput! Done! No more drip! Kind of sad that the clock still works though.

Who's at the wheel? (1)

It was a beautiful fall day. I was in the little town of Boonsboro, MD.

I had just had a lovely get together with a friend I had not seen since before covid.

(at least 18-20 months)

It was time to go home. I was filled with gratitude and love.

I went to the GPS and asked for directions back to Cumberland MD.

I had two choices. I picked the shorter journey. Once I was on my way, I realized the GPS gave me a longer journey. I was cursing out loud and angry that I noticed it too late. It was going to take me 45 more minutes to get home. Man, was I pissed and a bit impatient.

I surrendered. I began to see the sky~the clouds in the lovely setting sun.

I began to see the trees and the foliage. I started to enjoy the journey.

Time passed in beauty. The road was winding. The fields, trees and sky kept giving me glimpses of my inner journey…With the music playing, I said out loud:

"I let go of my shame!! I release my shame!!"

Bam. I came around the corner, and there in front of me was a sign placed before crossing a creek. It said "The Devil's Backbone."

I laughed out loud…I thought, I have left my shame on the Devil's Backbone.

He can have it, I thought. Good riddance! No more shame to carry.

Who was at the wheel that day?

Who's at the wheel? (Second time.)

It was a cool, clear and sunny winter afternoon. I was returning from a trip to the Pittsburgh Airport.

Once again the GPS put me on to the winding roads of Pennsylvania.

I decided to let it go. I turned up my music. I was playing Queen. I was swooshing around the curves. Then, my Pandora shut down and immediately turned back on to another station.

It was "Maneesh." I chuckled and said out loud: "Okay"...Then, my feet went to the brakes and I went from 60 MPH to 20 MPH in an instant. Around that next curve was a warning sign regarding the 20 MPH along with other caution signs. Who knows what would have happened if I had been speeding around that corner. I then took in the beautiful mellow sounds and slowly traveled through the fields of Pennsylvania a tad slower than 20 MPH.
(Why I didn't take pictures, I don't know.)

As I entered Maryland, the Pandora music shifted off then again back on.

This time it was the Singing Bowls. I let it stay on the high-pitched sound.

WHOOOAMMMMM...A deep resonant sound of a bell came in...It vibrated my whole car, the seat I was sitting in, the wheel with my hands, the floorboard with my feet. My whole body hummed. My flesh and bones vibrated to this earthly deep low pitch. I stopped my car and sat for 15 minutes letting the sound wash through me. I was feeling as if something greater than me was running through me. I surrendered to the fantastical movements of thoughts, flesh, bone, and blood that were all in sync to the vehicle and the Bluetooth noise.

I felt as if I just had a wonderful loving bath, and a full body massage after some incredibly intense love making.

My friend called it Divine Intervention.

Who was at the wheel that day?

Eternity in a moment

That place just before the final exhale is a curiosity I desire to postpone. (Though I know, it could be in any minute now.)

Yet, with a serenity greater than my mind,

I dance as if it is far beyond this time.

I breathe in, to place it even further up the road.

For now, I do my best to clean up my purgatory.

And have the spark of joy light my path.

Last word from

The Defiant Gardener

"Empathy in our connection to nature ensures our survival. Compassion for connection and others can guarantee future generations a glimpse of the whole world that carries us."

"According to our stories, we were once in the garden. We can claim our journey back and revel in its mystery by allowing our communities to celebrate and conserve its majesty."

"Our common connection is our planet. The sooner we stop raping it, exploiting it, and destroying it, the better for all of us and our progeny. The sooner all of us become protectors, the better our chance for the survival of all species."

This may end. Yet, in the cosmos we live in, we will forever be.

Surviving has led me into ELDERHOOD.

Mind you, it hasn't been without rebellion. I have actually wrestled with surviving...I have kicked, screamed, drank, radiated my inner organs and ingested pharmaceuticals to survive. I have slept over in the slumbered stage of youth..It has actually, at times, dragged me kicking and screaming..I then get a foothold and run back to "the once was", which is now "a never again"..

Oh , and the work, mind you...Lots of inner work.

Finally, I am in Elderhood....Oh my, I can not deny it...It is like putting on a new suit and tie..

I have not worn a suit and tie for decades..Do you mind if I create my own attire?

...Pardon me if it takes a little time for me to acclimate but I will whip together an outfit to die for.

Elderhood, Okay, so surviving has taught me many things, and I am now at your threshold ready for service..

Gratitude and Joy are my accouterments...Whimsy is my regalia. And Love is what brought me here.

.

SAYING THE UNSPEAKABLE

When I have reached the end of this life, do not be sad.

For I have seen earth BLOOM.

Do not shed a tear. For I have crawled in the gutter and danced on the mountain top.

I have seen myself in many valleys and have dropped down from the clouds.

I have shied away from the sun, but oh how the moonlight has held my heart like a pendulum.

I have had rages like a pent-up bull and sighed like a summer breeze with fireflies.

Yes, do not carry a mournful heart. For I have been blessed with many beginnings and endings.

This is simply just another one. Another ending and another beginning.

I ask that you rejoice in my departure. For the being that I was, and for the being I am now, is eternally whispering life's glorious existence.

Bring your head up and walk with the knowledge that at times, our friendship was true.

And that no matter what others say, for once the truth is exposed, it changes like a passing of a life.

I have passed my friend, I continue to live happily ever after.

Yes, the world calls out to you now.

Listen. There are such wondrous things to behold.

Mission

I teach and remind humans to appreciate our planet by visiting and showing gardens and landscapes around the globe along with offering inspirational words from people that encourage preservation for our common world. (And for the many worlds we have in common.)

Me

I am a queer, cisgender man born mid-twentieth century. I am a landscape gardener and garden artist who explores the terrain of words and other forms of art.

I have been published in smaller collections of works over the years. This is my first endeavor in creating a chapbook for me and for you…

मैं अपनी यह पुस्तक अपने ज्येष्ठ पुत्र आशीष श्रीवास्तव को समर्पित करता हूँ जिसने मुझे डिजिटल मार्केटिंग के विषय विशेष पर ज्ञानवर्धक पुस्तक लिखने के लिए प्रेरित किया।